TRADITIONAL SONGS FOR BEGINNING GUITAR

by PETER PENHALLOW

Editor: Jeffrey Pepper Rodgers

Cover photograph: Rory Earnshaw

Author photograph: Ross Pelton

ISBN: 978-0-6340-7793-7

STRING LETTER PUBLISHING

EXCLUSIVELY DISTRIBUTED BY

HAL•LEONARD®
CORPORATION

7777 W. BLUEMOUND RD. P.O. BOX 13819 MILWAUKEE, WI 53213

Visit Hal Leonard Online at
www.halleonard.com

In Australia Contact:
Hal Leonard Australia Pty. Ltd.
4 Lentara Court
Cheltenham, Victoria, 3192 Australia
Email: ausadmin@halleonard.com

CONTENTS

INTRODUCTION

In this songbook are 15 of your favorite traditional songs, arranged for beginning guitar. You'll learn easy versions of both the melody and rhythm parts, so you can play these songs as guitar instrumentals or accompany singing (the complete lyrics are included for each song). The chords, keys, and techniques used are all taught in Book One of *The Acoustic Guitar Method.*

Perhaps the easiest songs in this collection are "He's Got the Whole World in His Hands" and "Rock My Soul," which use only two chords each. Many more songs ("Amazing Grace," "Michael, Row Your Boat Ashore," "Swing Low, Sweet Chariot," "Down by the Riverside," "Kumbaya," "This Train," and "When the Saints Go Marching In") use just three or four chords. "Will the Circle Be Unbroken," "Home on the Range," "This Little Light of Mine," and "I've Got Peace Like a River" feature slightly more complex chord structures. "Sometimes I Feel Like a Motherless Child" and "When Johnny Comes Marching Home" are both in minor

keys, which we will discuss along the way. The kinds of chords, chord progressions, rhythm, and melodies used in these songs are fundamental to countless styles of traditional guitar music.

The CD includes five tracks for each song. The first two tracks illustrate the accompaniment pattern (up to tempo and slowly). Then I play the full song as an instrumental (again, up to tempo and slowly) and, finally, sing a verse over the rhythm guitar. The instrumental versions on the CD are recorded with the rhythm guitar on the left and the guitar melody on the right. You can pan your stereo left or right if you want to isolate the lead or rhythm.

Playing at the slower tempo is a great way to program the moves, enabling you to gradually come up to speed. With a little practice, you should soon be entertaining your friends and family with these great traditional songs. Have fun.

—*Peter Penhallow*

Introduction
and Tune-Up

TRACK
1

Need help with the songs in this book? Ask a question in our free, on-line support forum in the Guitar Talk section of www.acousticguitar.com.

MUSIC NOTATION KEY

The music in this book is written in standard notation and tablature. Here's how to read it.

STANDARD NOTATION

Standard notation is written on a five-line staff. Notes are written in alphabetical order from A to G.

The duration of a note is determined by three things: the note head, stem, and flag. A whole note (○) equals four beats. A half note (♩) is half of that: two beats. A quarter note (♩) equals one beat, an eighth note (♪) equals half of one beat, and a 16th note (♬) is a quarter beat (there are four 16th notes per beat).

The fraction (4/4, 3/4, 6/8, etc.) or ¢ character shown at the beginning of a piece of music denotes the time signature. The top number tells you how many beats are in each measure, and the bottom number indicates the rhythmic value of each beat (4 equals a quarter note, 8 equals an eighth note, 16 equals a 16th note, and 2 equals a half note). The most common time signature is 4/4, which signifies four quarter notes per measure and is sometimes designated with the symbol ¢ (for common time). The symbol ¢ stands for cut time (2/2). Most songs are in either 4/4 or 3/4.

TABLATURE

In tablature, the six horizontal lines represent the six strings of the guitar, with the first string on the top and sixth on the bottom. The numbers refer to fret numbers on a given string. The notation and tablature in this book are designed to be used in tandem—refer to the notation to get the rhythmic information and note durations, and refer to the tablature to get the exact locations of the notes on the guitar fingerboard.

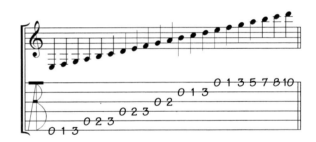

FINGERINGS

Fingerings are indicated with small numbers and letters in the notation. Fretting-hand fingering is indicated with 1 for the index finger, 2 the middle, 3 the ring, 4 the fourth finger, and *T* the thumb. Picking-hand fingering is indicated by *i* for the index finger, *m* the middle, *a* the ring, *c* the fourth finger, and *p* the thumb. Remember that the fingerings indicated are only suggestions; if you find a different way that works better for you, use it.

CHORD DIAGRAMS

Chord diagrams show where the fingers go on the fingerboard. Frets are shown horizontally, and the thick top line represents the nut. The sixth (lowest-pitched) string is on the far left, and the first (highest-pitched) string is on the far right. Dots show where the fingers go, and the numbers above the diagram tell you which fretting-hand fingers to use: 1 for the index finger, 2 the middle, 3 the ring, 4 the fourth finger, and T the thumb. An X indicates a string that should be muted or not played; 0 indicates an open string.

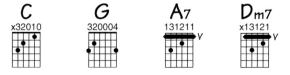

CAPOS

If a capo is used, a Roman numeral indicates the fret where the capo should be placed. The standard notation and tablature is written as if the capo were the nut of the guitar. For instance, a tune capoed anywhere up the neck and played using key-of-G chord shapes and fingerings will be written in the key of G. Likewise, open strings held down by the capo are written as open strings.

TUNINGS

Alternate guitar tunings are given from the lowest (sixth) string to the highest (first) string. For instance, D A D G B E indicates standard tuning with the bottom string dropped to D. Standard notation for songs in alternate tunings always reflects the actual pitches of the notes. Arrows underneath tuning notes indicate strings that are altered from standard tuning and whether they are tuned up or down.

VOCAL TUNES

Vocal tunes are sometimes written with a fully tabbed-out introduction and a vocal melody with chord diagrams for the rest of the piece. The tab intro is usually your indication of which strum or fingerpicking pattern to use in the rest of the piece. The melody with lyrics underneath is the melody sung by the vocalist. Occasionally smaller notes are written with the melody to indicate the harmony part sung by another vocalist. These are not to be confused with cue notes, which are small notes that indicate melodies that vary when a section is repeated. Listen to a recording of the piece to get a feel for the guitar accompaniment and to hear the singing if you aren't skilled at reading vocal melodies.

ARTICULATIONS

There are a number of ways you can articulate a note on the guitar. Notes connected with slurs (not to be confused with ties) in the tablature or standard notation are articulated with a hammer-on, a pull-off, or a slide. Lower notes slurred to higher notes are played as hammer-ons; higher notes slurred to lower notes are played as pull-offs. While it's usually obvious that slurred notes are played as hammer-ons or pull-offs, an H or P is included above the tablature as an extra reminder.

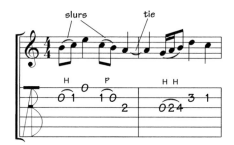

Slides are represented with a dash, and an S is included above the tab. A dash preceding a note represents a slide into the note from an indefinite point in the direction of the slide; a dash following a note indicates a slide off of the note to an indefinite point in the direction of the slide. For two slurred notes connected with a slide, you should pick the first note and then slide into the second.

Bends are represented with upward curves, as shown in the next example. Most bends have a specific destination pitch—the number above the bend symbol shows how much the bend raises the string's pitch: $^1/_4$ for a slight bend, $^1/_2$ for a half step, 1 for a whole step.

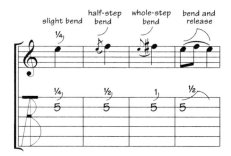

Grace notes are represented by small notes with a dash through the stem in standard notation and with small numbers in the tab. A grace note is a very quick ornament leading into a note, most commonly executed as a hammer-on, pull-off, or slide. In the following example, pluck the note at the fifth fret on the beat, then quickly hammer onto the seventh fret. The second example is executed as a quick pull-off from the second fret to the open string. In the third example, both notes at the fifth fret are played simultaneously (even though it appears that the fifth fret, fourth string, is to be played by itself), then the seventh fret, fourth string, is quickly hammered.

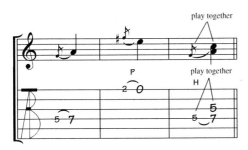

HARMONICS

Harmonics are represented by diamond-shaped notes in the standard notation and a small dot next to the tablature numbers. Natural harmonics are indicated with the text "Harmonics" or "Harm." above the tablature. Harmonics articulated with the right hand (often called artificial harmonics) include the text "R.H. Harmonics" or "R.H. Harm." above the tab. Right-hand harmonics are executed by lightly touching the harmonic note (usually 12 frets above the open string or fretted note) with the right-hand index finger and plucking the string with the thumb or ring finger or pick. For extended phrases played with right-hand harmonics, the fretted notes are shown in the tab along with instructions to touch the harmonics 12 fret above the notes.

REPEATS

One of the most confusing parts of a musical score can be the navigation symbols, such as repeats, *D.S. al Coda*, *D.C. al Fine*, *To Coda*, etc.

Repeat symbols are placed at the beginning and end of the passage to be repeated.

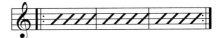

You should ignore repeat symbols with the dots on the right side the first time you encounter them; when you come to a repeat symbol with dots on the left side, jump back to the previous repeat symbol facing the opposite direction (if there is no previous symbol, go to the beginning of the piece). The next time you come to the repeat symbol, ignore it and keep going unless it includes instructions such as "Repeat three times."

Often a section will often have a different ending after each repeat. The example below includes a first and a second ending. Play until you hit the repeat symbol, jump back to the previous repeat symbol and play until you reach the bracketed first ending, skip the measures under the bracket and jump immediately to the second ending, and then continue.

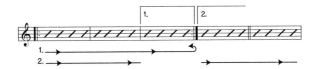

D.S. stands for *dal segno* or "from the sign." When you encounter this indication, jump immediately to the sign (𝄋). *D.S.* is usually accompanied by *al Fine* or *al Coda*. *Fine* indicates the end of a piece. A coda is a final passage near the end of a piece and is indicated with ⊕. *D.S. al Coda* simply tells you to jump back to the sign and continue on until you are instructed to jump to the coda, indicated with *To Coda* ⊕.

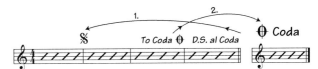

D.C. stands for *da capo* or "from the beginning." Jump to the top of the piece when you encounter this indication.

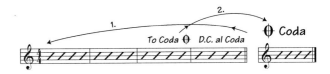

D.C. al Fine tells you to jump to the beginning of a tune and continue until you encounter the *Fine* indicating the end of the piece (ignore the *Fine* the first time through).

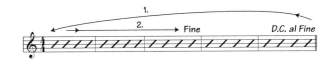

AMAZING GRACE

John Newton was a minister who wrote the words to many hymns, the most familiar being "Amazing Grace." A former slave trader, Newton intimated that his words were self-reflective: "I once was lost, and now I'm found."

This song is one of my all-time faves. Ray Charles sings a knock-out version on the various-artists collection *Music of Hope* (Tim Janus Ensemble 1901). You can hear a nice acoustic performance on *The Pizza Tapes* (Acoustic Disc 41), featuring David Grisman on mandolin, Jerry Garcia on guitar and vocals, and Tony Rice on guitar.

This is basically a three-chord arrangement (using A, D, and E), but note that over the word *lost* the A switches to an A7. The A7 spices up the progression a bit and underscores the change to the D chord.

TRACK **2** Accompaniment Pattern   TRACK **3** Played Slowly

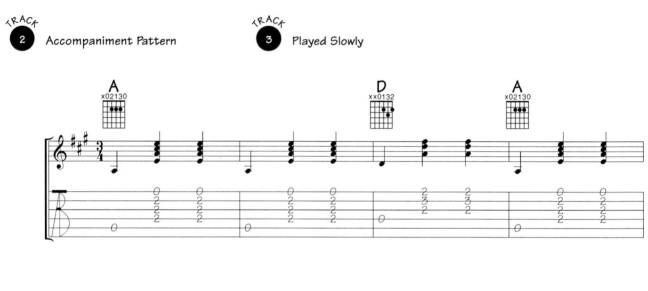

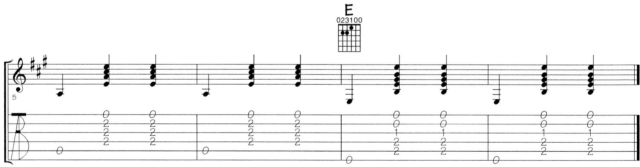

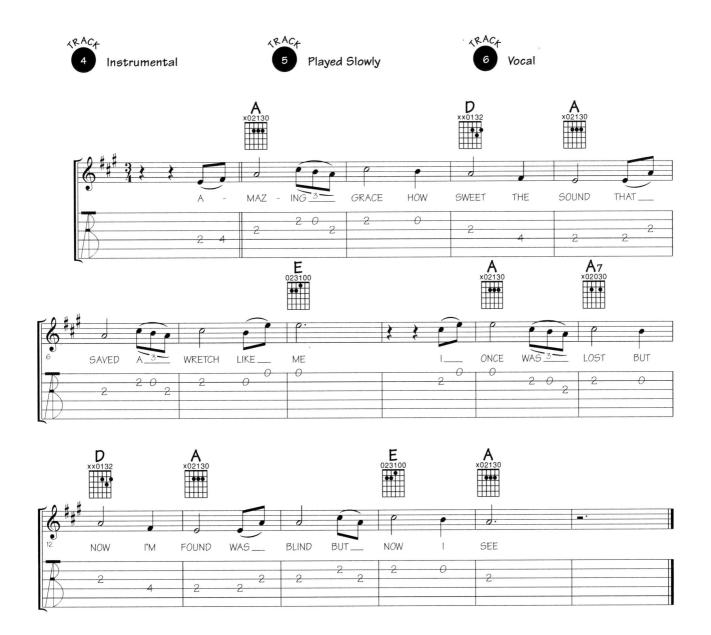

1. A   D   A
   AMAZING GRACE HOW SWEET THE SOUND
                    E
   THAT SAVED A WRETCH LIKE ME
     A   A7   D   A
   I ONCE WAS LOST, BUT NOW I'M FOUND
               E   A
   WAS BLIND, BUT NOW I SEE

2.   D   A
   'TWAS GRACE THAT TAUGHT MY HEART TO FEAR
                 E
   AND GRACE MY FEAR RELIEVED
      A   A7   D   A
   HOW PRECIOUS DID THAT GRACE APPEAR
             E   A
   THE HOUR I FIRST BELIEVED

3.   D   A
   THROUGH MANY DANGERS, TOILS, AND SNARES
               E
   WE HAVE ALREADY COME
          A   A7   D   A
   'TWAS GRACE THAT BROUGHT US SAFE THUS FAR
                E
   AND GRACE WILL LEAD US HOME

HE'S GOT THE WHOLE WORLD IN HIS HANDS

Like "Amazing Grace," this tune is in the key of A, but it uses only two chords: A and E7. That E7 is an essential chord for blues as well as many other styles of roots music.

If there is a central source of music, it is what musicians like to refer to as the groove. Think of the groove as not just the tempo but the feel of a song. "He's Got the Whole World in His Hands" has a very laid-back groove. So get into the groove!

Ella Jenkins sings a nice guitar and vocal arrangement of this tune, with some kids backing her up, on *Little Johnny Brown and Other Songs* (Smithsonian Folkways 45026).

TRACK 7 Accompaniment Pattern   **TRACK 8** Played Slowly

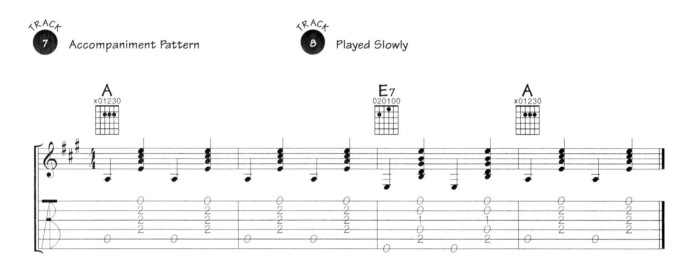

TRACK 9 Instrumental   **TRACK 10** Played Slowly   **TRACK 11** Vocal

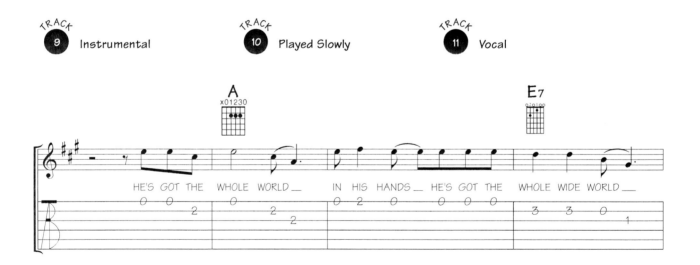

1.   A
    HE'S GOT THE WHOLE WORLD IN HIS HANDS
          E7   A
    HE'S GOT THE WHOLE WIDE WORLD IN HIS HANDS

    HE'S GOT THE WHOLE WORLD IN HIS HANDS
          E7   A
    HE'S GOT THE WHOLE WORLD IN HIS HANDS

2.   HE'S GOT THE WIND AND THE RAIN IN HIS HANDS
          E7   A
    HE'S GOT THE WIND AND THE RAIN IN HIS HANDS

    HE'S GOT THE WIND AND THE RAIN IN HIS HANDS
          E7   A
    HE'S GOT THE WHOLE WORLD IN HIS HANDS

3.   HE'S GOT THE SUN AND THE MOON IN HIS HANDS
          E7   A
    HE'S GOT THE SUN AND THE MOON IN HIS HANDS

    HE'S GOT THE SUN AND THE MOON IN HIS HANDS
          E7   A
    HE'S GOT THE WHOLE WORLD IN HIS HANDS

4.   HE'S GOT THE LITTLE BITTY BABY IN HIS HANDS
          E7   A
    HE'S GOT THE LITTLE BITTY BABY IN HIS HANDS

    HE'S GOT THE LITTLE BITTY BABY IN HIS HANDS
          E7   A
    HE'S GOT THE WHOLE WORLD IN HIS HANDS

5.   HE'S GOT YOU AND ME, BROTHER, IN HIS HANDS
        E7   A
    HE'S GOT YOU AND ME, BROTHER, IN HIS HANDS

    HE'S GOT YOU AND ME, BROTHER, IN HIS HANDS
          E7   A
    HE'S GOT THE WHOLE WORLD IN HIS HANDS

6.   HE'S GOT EVERYBODY HERE IN HIS HANDS
          E7   A
    HE'S GOT EVERYBODY HERE IN HIS HANDS

    HE'S GOT EVERYBODY HERE IN HIS HANDS
          E7   A
    HE'S GOT THE WHOLE WORLD IN HIS HANDS

MICHAEL, ROW YOUR BOAT ASHORE

It is said that the shore in this song is the shore of the Jordan river, and that Michael is St. Michael, who guides us at least metaphorically, if not at one time literally, to the Jordan shore. Music historians have noted that slaves sang this song in hopes of safely reaching the shore of the Mississippi, where they were assisted in their escape by ferry.

I enjoyed "Michael" at age seven when the Highwaymen made this wonderful spiritual a big hit on the radio. You can hear their version on *Michael, Row the Boat Ashore: The Best of the Highwaymen* (Capitol 96334).

"Michael" uses a three-chord progression, this time in D (D, G, A7). In music theory, progressions can be expressed with Roman numerals. In the key of D, the D chord is I, the G chord is IV, and the A chord is V. The I is your home chord, where you begin your journey. You travel to the IV and V, and when you arrive back at I, your boat has reached the shore!

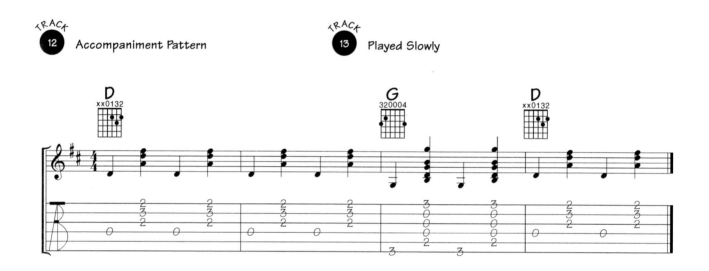

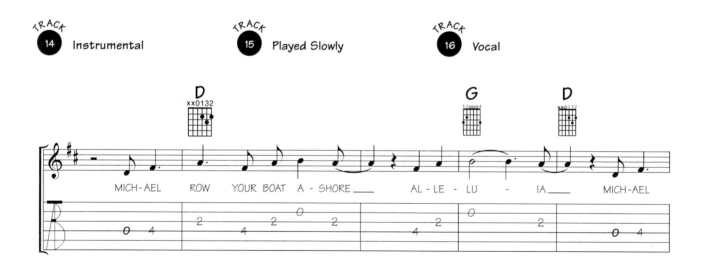

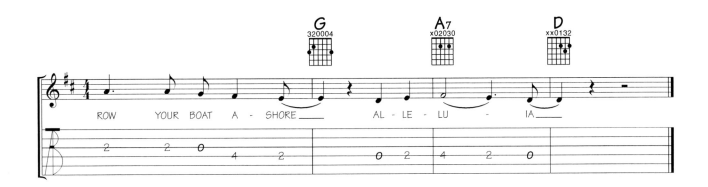

ROW   YOUR BOAT   A - SHORE____   AL - LE - LU - IA____

1. MICHAEL, ROW YOUR BOAT ASHORE, ALLELUIA
   MICHAEL, ROW YOUR BOAT ASHORE, ALLELUIA

2. SISTER, HELP TO TRIM THE SAIL, ALLELUIA
   SISTER, HELP TO TRIM THE SAIL, ALLELUIA

3. THE RIVER JORDAN IS DEEP AND WIDE, ALLELUIA
   MILK AND HONEY ON THE OTHER SIDE, ALLELUIA

4. THE RIVER JORDAN IS CHILLY AND COLD, ALLELUIA
   CHILLS THE BODY BUT NOT THE SOUL, ALLELUIA

5. THEN YOU'LL FEAR THE TRUMPET SOUND, ALLELUIA
   SINNER, ROW TO SAVE YOUR SOUL, ALLELUIA

SWING LOW, SWEET CHARIOT

"**C**hariot" was a metaphor for any vehicle used to transport runaway slaves, such as ferry or train or the Underground Railroad. The song itself is also a vehicle that carries us home, to the good feeling that music brings to us.

"Swing Low" uses a three-chord progression, once again in the key of A (A, D, E7). Johnny Cash delivers the goods with a deep and emotional performance on the compilation *Your Favorite Country Hymns* (Ranwood 7044).

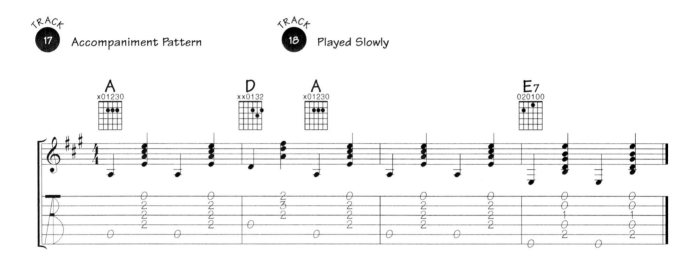

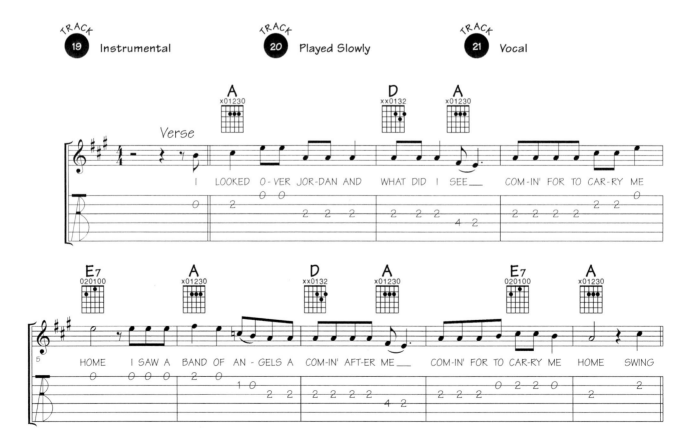

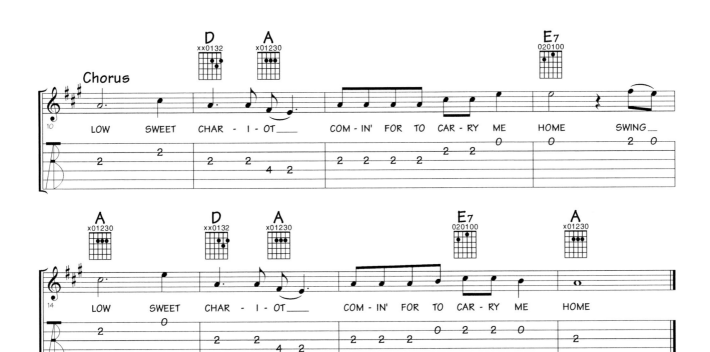

A
1. I LOOKED OVER JORDAN
     D   A
   AND WHAT DID I SEE
                      E7
   COMIN' FOR TO CARRY ME HOME
          A   D   A
   I SAW A BAND OF ANGELS A COMIN' AFTER ME
          E7   A
   COMIN' FOR TO CARRY ME HOME

                 D   A
   SWING LOW, SWEET CHARIOT
                   E7
   COMIN' FOR TO CARRY ME HOME
          A   D   A
   SWING LOW, SWEET CHARIOT
          E7   A
   COMIN' FOR TO CARRY ME HOME

                 D   A
2. IF YOU GET THERE BEFORE I DO
                   E7
   COMIN' FOR TO CARRY ME HOME
          A   D   A
   TELL ALL MY FRIENDS I'M COMIN' TOO
          E7   A
   COMIN' FOR TO CARRY ME HOME

      CHORUS

3. SOMETIMES I'M UP
           D   A
   AND SOMETIMES I'M DOWN
                        E7
   COMIN' FOR TO CARRY ME HOME
          A
   BUT STILL MY SOUL
          D   A
   FEELS HEAVENLY BOUND
          E7   A
   COMIN' FOR TO CARRY ME HOME

      CHORUS

WILL THE CIRCLE BE UNBROKEN

Words by Ada R. Haberson • Music by Charles H. Gabriel

"**W**ill the Circle Be Unbroken" is in the key of G. Notice that the G sometimes shifts to G7 before moving to the next chord. The progression is an unbroken circle in itself: expressed in Roman numerals, the song goes from I to IV (C) and V (D) and back to I (G).

When you're playing "Will the Circle Be Unbroken"—

especially with other people—try to maintain the groove and keep the beat. It's always a good thing not to break the circle!

Master flatpicker and folksinger extraordinaire Doc Watson performs this song with down-home authenticity on *Original Folkways Recordings: 1960–1962* (Smithsonian Folkways 40023/30).

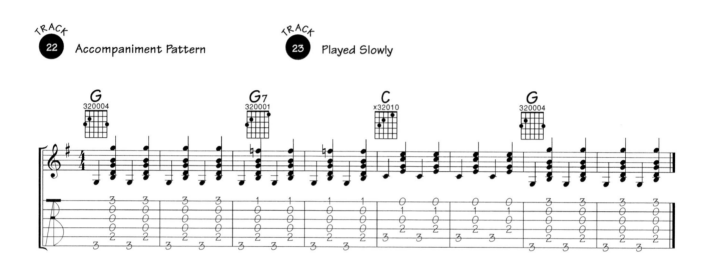

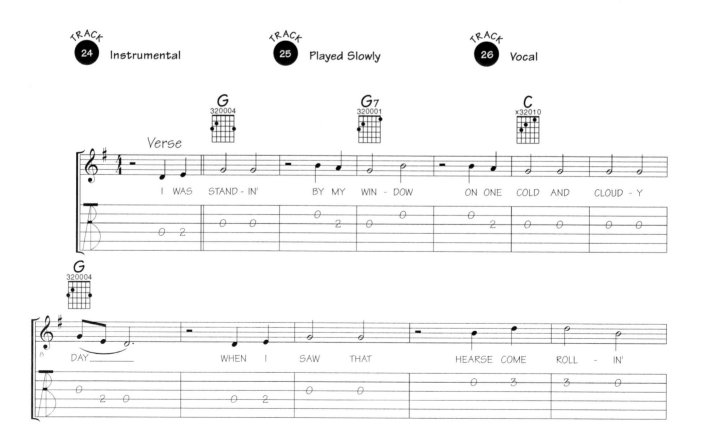

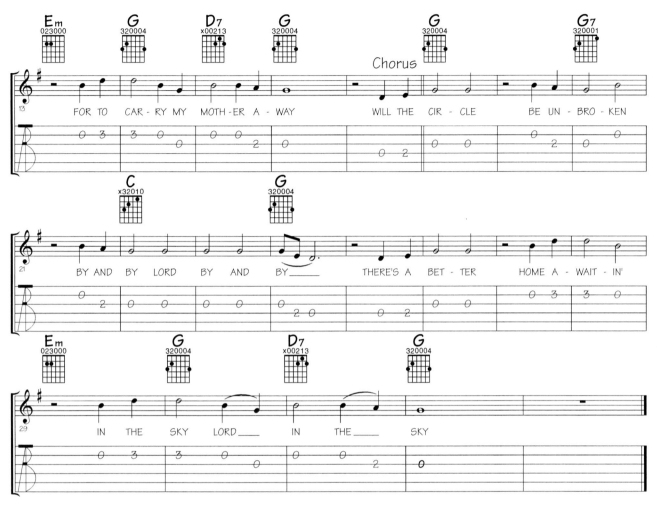

1. I WAS STANDIN' BY MY WINDOW
   G   *G7*
   ON ONE COLD AND CLOUDY DAY
   C   *G*
   WHEN I SAW THAT HEARSE COME ROLLIN'
                              Em
   FOR TO CARRY MY MOTHER AWAY
   G   *D7*   *G*

   WILL THE CIRCLE BE UNBROKEN
                    G7
   BY AND BY, LORD, BY AND BY
      C   *G*
   THERE'S A BETTER HOME AWAITIN'
                              Em
   IN THE SKY, LORD, IN THE SKY
   G   *D7*   *G*

2. I SAID TO THAT UNDERTAKER
                       G7
   UNDERTAKER, PLEASE DRIVE SLOW
      C   *G*
   FOR THIS LADY YOU ARE CARRYING
                              Em
   LORD, I HATE TO SEE HER GO
   G   *D7*   *G*

   CHORUS

3. OH, I FOLLOWED CLOSE BEHIND HER
                               G7
   TRIED TO HOLD UP AND BE BRAVE
      C   *G*
   BUT I COULD NOT HIDE MY SORROW
                              Em
   WHEN THEY LAID HER IN THE GRAVE
   G   *D7*   *G*

   CHORUS

4. I WENT BACK HOME, MY HOME WAS LONESOME
                                       G7
   MISSED MY MOTHER, SHE WAS GONE
      C   *G*
   ALL OF MY BROTHERS, SISTERS CRYING
                              Em
   WHAT A HOME, SO SAD AND LONE
   G   *D7*   *G*

   CHORUS

HOME ON THE RANGE

Daniel E. Kelly, fiddler and construction worker, wrote the music to "Home on the Range" in 1873. Kelly's niece Ginnie helped write the words, inspired by "Western Home," a poem written by Dr. Brewster Higley in 1871. "Home on the Range" became the state song of Kansas in 1947.

The song can be played as a three-chord progression in G, but the addition of the A7 helps to make it interesting. As

your playing develops, you'll learn many ways to embellish simple progressions. The chorus also includes a very common progression of Em to A7 to D7.

I can't sing this song without thinking of the classic Roy Rogers and the Sons of the Pioneers version, which you can hear on *Roy Rogers and Dale Evans/Sons of the Pioneers* (Camden 6094).

TRACK 27 Accompaniment Pattern   **TRACK 28** Played Slowly

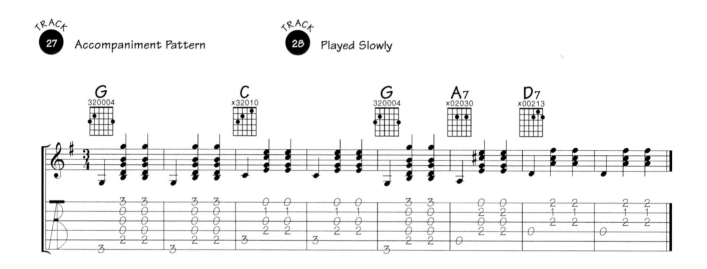

TRACK 29 Instrumental   **TRACK 30** Played Slowly   **TRACK 31** Vocal

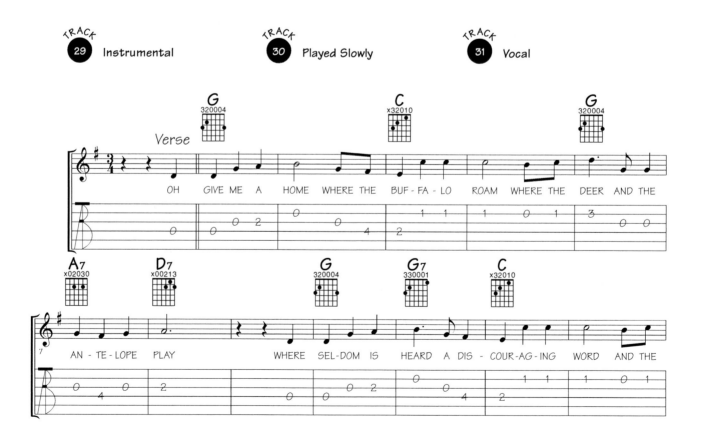

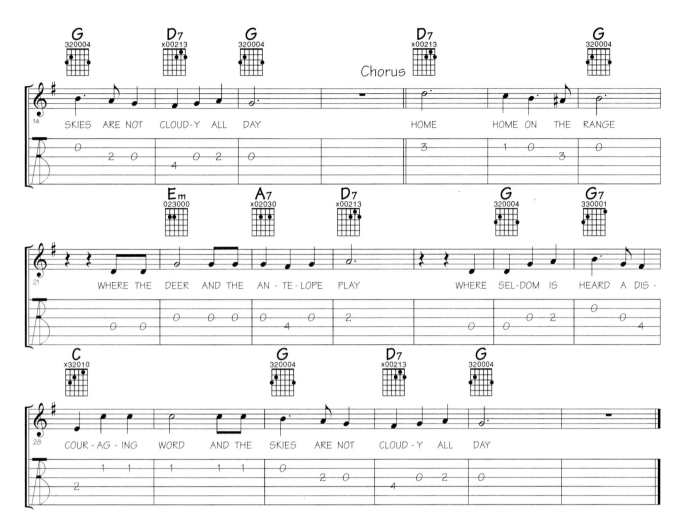

G
1. OH, GIVE ME A HOME WHERE THE BUFFALO ROAM
       G   A7   D7
  WHERE THE DEER AND THE ANTELOPE PLAY
       G   G7   C
  WHERE SELDOM IS HEARD A DISCOURAGING WORD
         G   D7   G
  AND THE SKIES ARE NOT CLOUDY ALL DAY

  D7   G
  HOME, HOME ON THE RANGE
           Em   A7   D7
  WHERE THE DEER AND THE ANTELOPE PLAY
       G   G7   C
  WHERE SELDOM IS HEARD A DISCOURAGING WORD
        G   D7   G
  AND THE SKIES ARE NOT CLOUDY ALL DAY

               G   C
2. HOW OFTEN AT NIGHT WHEN THE HEAVENS ARE BRIGHT
         G   A7   D7
  WITH THE LIGHT FROM THE GLITTERING STARS
        G   G7   C
  HAVE I STOOD THERE AMAZED AND ASKED AS I GAZED
        G   D7   G
  IF THEIR GLORY EXCEEDS THAT OF OURS

    CHORUS

                                      C
3. WHERE THE AIR IS SO PURE, THE ZEPHYRS SO FREE
       G   A7   D7
  THE BREEZES SO BALMY AND LIGHT
       G   G7   C
  THAT I WOULD NOT EXCHANGE MY HOME ON THE RANGE
        G   D7   G
  FOR ALL OF THE CITIES SO BRIGHT

    CHORUS

DOWN BY THE RIVERSIDE

I'm gonna lay down the bummers of the day, down by the riverside, and get into the groove of guitar practice. And I ain't a gonna study war no more!

Notice that the verse of "Down by the Riverside" is a simple two-chord progression, from G to D7. The bridge,

however, adds the IV chord (C), creating a three-chord progression in the key of G.

Elvis Presley combined gospel with rock in his rousing arrangement on *Peace in the Valley: The Complete Gospel Recordings* (RCA 67991).

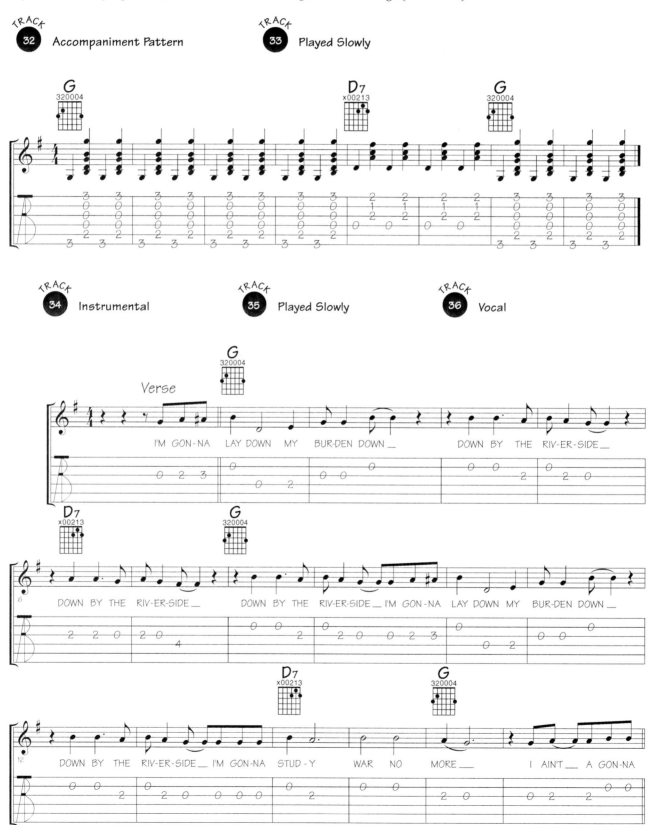

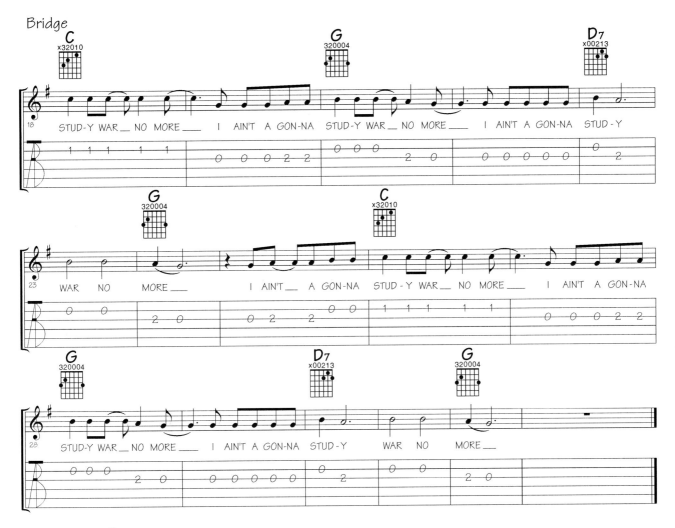

1. G
    I'M GONNA LAY DOWN MY BURDEN, DOWN

    DOWN BY THE RIVERSIDE
    D7   G
    DOWN BY THE RIVERSIDE, DOWN BY THE RIVERSIDE

    I'M GONNA LAY DOWN MY BURDEN, DOWN

    DOWN BY THE RIVERSIDE
            D7   G
    I'M GONNA STUDY WAR NO MORE

                    C
        I AIN'T A GONNA STUDY WAR NO MORE
                    G
        I AIN'T A GONNA STUDY WAR NO MORE
                        D7   G
        I AIN'T A GONNA STUDY WAR NO MORE
                    C
        I AIN'T A GONNA STUDY WAR NO MORE
                    G
        I AIN'T A GONNA STUDY WAR NO MORE
                        D7   G
        I AIN'T A GONNA STUDY WAR NO MORE

2. WELL, I'M GONNA PUT ON MY LONG WHITE ROBE

    DOWN BY THE RIVERSIDE
    D7   G
    DOWN BY THE RIVERSIDE, DOWN BY THE RIVERSIDE

    I'M GONNA PUT ON MY LONG WHITE ROBE

    DOWN BY THE RIVERSIDE
                    D7   G
    I'M GONNA STUDY WAR NO MORE

        CHORUS

3. WELL, I'M GONNA LAY DOWN MY SWORD AND SHIELD

    DOWN BY THE RIVERSIDE
    D7   G
    DOWN BY THE RIVERSIDE, DOWN BY THE RIVERSIDE

    I'M GONNA LAY DOWN MY SWORD AND SHIELD

    DOWN BY THE RIVERSIDE
                    D7   G
    I'M GONNA STUDY WAR NO MORE

        CHORUS

KUMBAYA

"Kumbaya" was popular during the civil rights movement of the early 1960s. We wish for the greater good. We wish for emancipation and healing, which comes from, among other places, the power of music! This is the ultimate jam-around-the-campfire tune. In a jam session, we support each other, and the sum is greater than the parts. These ideas are universal and are reflected in the lyrics.

"Kumbaya" uses a three-chord progression in D (D, G, A7). Iconic folkster Joan Baez leads the jamboree on *Joan Baez in Concert, Part 1* (Vanguard 79598).

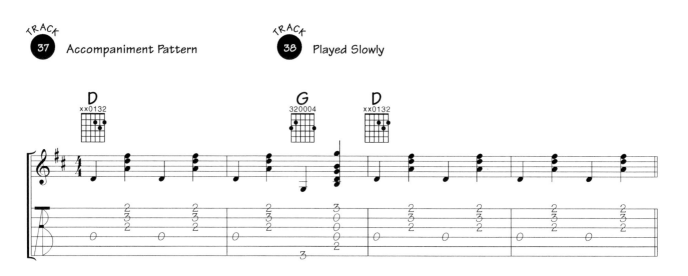

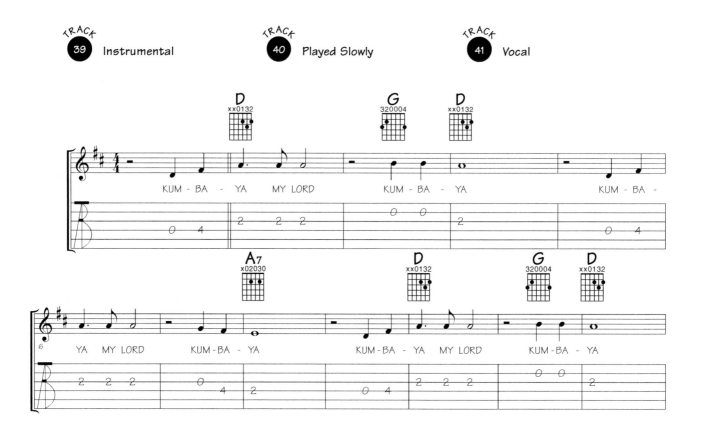

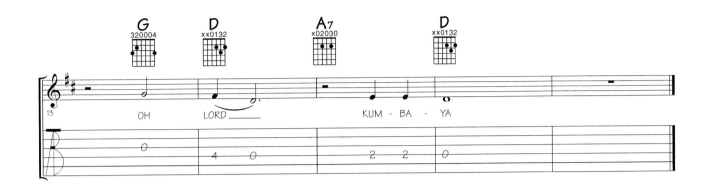

```
         D           G    D
KUMBAYA, MY LORD, KUMBAYA
                         A7
KUMBAYA, MY LORD, KUMBAYA
         D          G    D
KUMBAYA, MY LORD, KUMBAYA
G  D    A7    D
OH LORD, KUMBAYA
```

```
                        G    D
1. SOMEONE'S CRYING, LORD, KUMBAYA
                             A7
   SOMEONE'S CRYING, LORD, KUMBAYA
             D          G    D
   SOMEONE'S CRYING, LORD, KUMBAYA
   G  D    A7    D
   OH LORD, KUMBAYA
```

```
                        G    D
2. SOMEONE'S HUNGRY, LORD, KUMBAYA
                             A7
   SOMEONE'S HUNGRY, LORD, KUMBAYA
             D          G    D
   SOMEONE'S HUNGRY, LORD, KUMBAYA
   G  D    A7    D
   OH LORD, KUMBAYA
```

```
                        G    D
3. SOMEONE'S JOBLESS, LORD, KUMBAYA
                             A7
   SOMEONE'S JOBLESS, LORD, KUMBAYA
             D          G    D
   SOMEONE'S JOBLESS, LORD, KUMBAYA
   G  D    A7    D
   OH LORD, KUMBAYA
```

```
                           G    D
4. SOMEONE'S HURTING, LORD, KUMBAYA
                                A7
   SOMEONE'S HURTING, LORD, KUMBAYA
                D          G    D
   SOMEONE'S HURTING, LORD, KUMBAYA
   G  D    A7    D
   OH LORD, KUMBAYA
```

```
                            G    D
5. SOMEONE'S HOMELESS, LORD, KUMBAYA
                                 A7
   SOMEONE'S HOMELESS, LORD, KUMBAYA
                 D          G    D
   SOMEONE'S HOMELESS, LORD, KUMBAYA
   G  D    A7    D
   OH LORD, KUMBAYA
```

```
                           G    D
6. SOMEONE'S GREEDY, LORD, KUMBAYA
                                A7
   SOMEONE'S GREEDY, LORD, KUMBAYA
                D          G
   SOMEONE'S GREEDY, LORD, KUMBAYA
   G  D    A7    D
   OH LORD, KUMBAYA
```

```
                          G    D
7. COME BY HERE, MY LORD, KUMBAYA
                               A7
   COME BY HERE, MY LORD, KUMBAYA
               D          G    D
   COME BY HERE, MY LORD, KUMBAYA
   G  D    A7    D
   OH LORD, KUMBAYA
```

THIS TRAIN

I couldn't have omitted from this collection a song about trains. Kids of all ages, myself included, love train songs, so let's get into the chug-a-lug of this grooving train. Lonnie Donegan gives a classic performance on *More Than "Pye in the Sky"* (Bear Family 15700).

"This Train" features a simple three-chord progression in G (G, C, D7). It's easy to get lost when playing one chord

for so many measures—in this case, you play a G chord for six measures in a row. A good way to keep your bearings is learning to feel the natural cycle of four measures. In addition, the lyrics provide a useful clue: by the time the second lyric line comes around, four measures have passed, leaving only two more measures on the G chord before the change to D7.

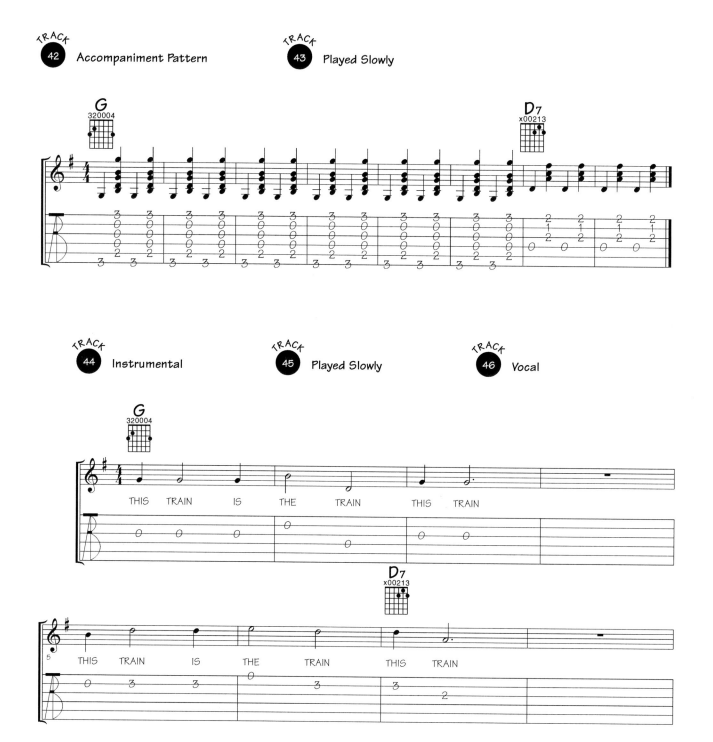

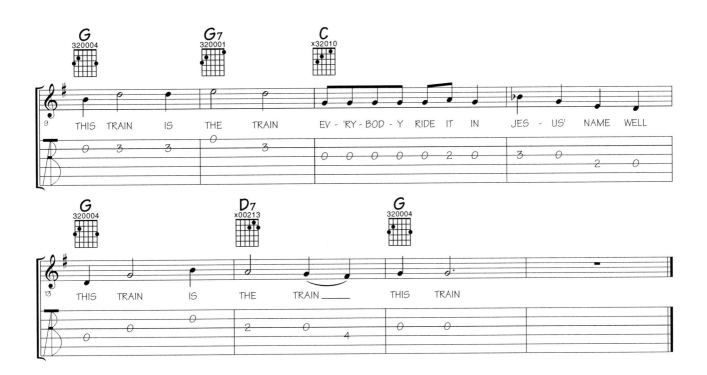

1.   G
THIS TRAIN IS THE TRAIN, THIS TRAIN
                          D7
THIS TRAIN IS THE TRAIN, THIS TRAIN
   G   G7
THIS TRAIN IS THE TRAIN
   C
EV'RYBODY RIDE IT IN JESUS' NAME, WELL
   G   D7   G
THIS TRAIN IS THE TRAIN, THIS TRAIN

2.   THIS TRAIN IS BOUND FOR GLORY, THIS TRAIN
                                D7
THIS TRAIN IS BOUND FOR GLORY, THIS TRAIN
   G   G7
THIS TRAIN IS BOUND FOR GLORY
   C
DON'T RIDE NOTHIN' BUT THE RIGHTEOUS AND HOLY
   G   D7   G
THIS TRAIN IS BOUND FOR GLORY, THIS TRAIN

3.   THIS TRAIN DON'T CARRY NO GAMBLERS, THIS TRAIN
                                  D7
THIS TRAIN DON'T CARRY NO GAMBLERS, THIS TRAIN
   G   G7
THIS TRAIN DON'T CARRY NO GAMBLERS
     C
NO HOT TOWN WOMEN, NO MIDNIGHT RAMBLERS
   G   D7   G
THIS TRAIN DON'T CARRY NO GAMBLERS, THIS TRAIN

4.   G
THIS TRAIN IS BUILT FOR SPEED NOW, THIS TRAIN
                              D7
THIS TRAIN IS BUILT FOR SPEED NOW, THIS TRAIN
   G   G7
THIS TRAIN IS BUILT FOR SPEED NOW
   C
FASTEST TRAIN YOU EVER DID SEE
   G   D7   G
THIS TRAIN IS BUILT FOR SPEED NOW, THIS TRAIN

5.   THIS TRAIN DON'T CARRY NO LIARS, THIS TRAIN
                              D7
THIS TRAIN DON'T CARRY NO LIARS, THIS TRAIN
   G   G7
THIS TRAIN DON'T CARRY NO LIARS
     C
NO HYPOCRITES AND NO HIGH FLYERS
   G   D7   G
THIS TRAIN DON'T CARRY NO LIARS, THIS TRAIN

6.   THIS TRAIN DON'T PAY NO TRANSPORTATION, THIS TRAIN
                                      D7
THIS TRAIN DON'T PAY NO TRANSPORTATION, THIS TRAIN
   G   G7
THIS TRAIN DON'T PAY NO TRANSPORTATION
   C
NO JIM CROW, NO DISCRIMINATION
   G   D7   G
THIS TRAIN DON'T PAY NO TRANSPORTATION, THIS TRAIN

THIS LITTLE LIGHT OF MINE

Like "Will the Circle Be Unbroken," "This Little Light of Mine" was a popular song in the '50s and '60s and was often sung at civil rights rallies. Brenda Lee, an original "girl singer" of that era, performs "This Little Light" in her inimitable country-pop style on *Country Gospel Classics* (Madacy Christian 50992). The Oak Ridge Boys lend their classic vocal harmonies to a nice modern country version on *Common Thread* (Word Entertainment 41185).

This song introduces B7, Em, and A7 chords, which serve to spice up this otherwise three-chord arrangement in G. The last eight bars can be a bit tricky, especially the quick change from G to B7. With practice, your fingers become so used to the shapes of the chords that these kinds of changes become automatic. If you're discouraged by your progress, sing, "This little light of mine, I'm gonna let it shine." Don't let anyone tell you otherwise.

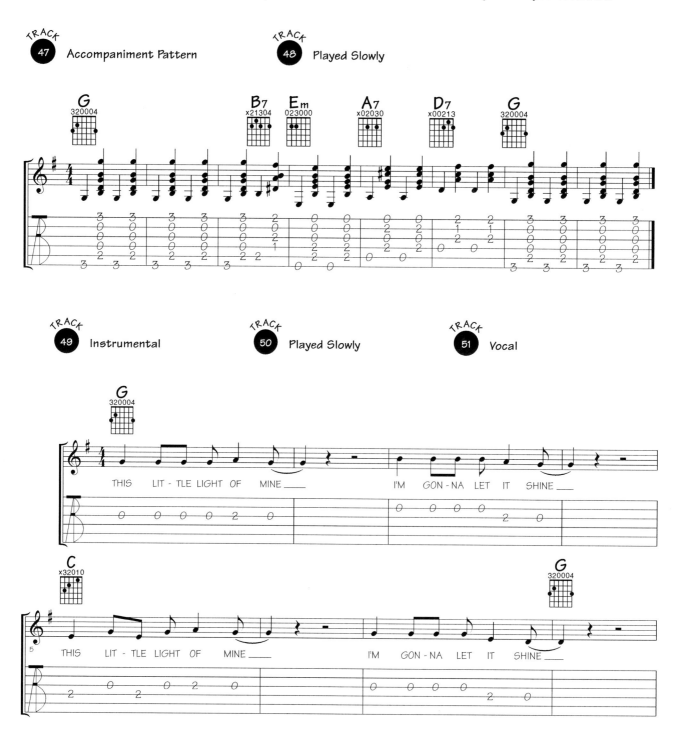

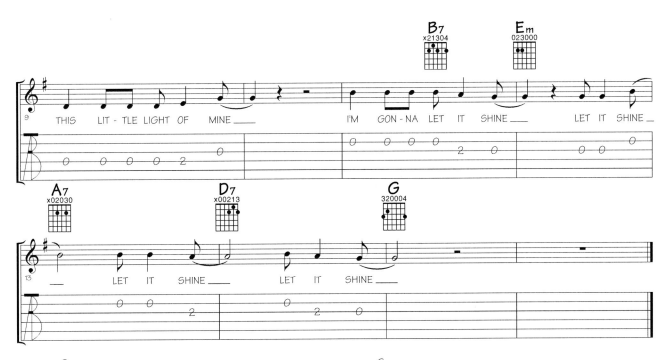

1. G
   THIS LITTLE LIGHT OF MINE

   I'M GONNA LET IT SHINE
   C
   THIS LITTLE LIGHT OF MINE
            G
   I'M GONNA LET IT SHINE

   THIS LITTLE LIGHT OF MINE
            B7   Em
   I'M GONNA LET IT SHINE
       A7   D7   G
   LET IT SHINE, LET IT SHINE, LET IT SHINE

2. HIDE IT UNDER A BUSHEL? NO!

   I'M GONNA LET IT SHINE
   C
   HIDE IT UNDER A BUSHEL? NO!
            G
   I'M GONNA LET IT SHINE

   HIDE IT UNDER A BUSHEL? NO!
            B7   Em
   I'M GONNA LET IT SHINE
       A7   D7   G
   LET IT SHINE, LET IT SHINE, LET IT SHINE

3. DON'T LET SATAN BLOW IT OUT

   I'M GONNA LET IT SHINE
   C
   DON'T LET SATAN BLOW IT OUT
            G
   I'M GONNA LET IT SHINE

   DON'T LET SATAN BLOW IT OUT
            B7   Em
   I'M GONNA LET IT SHINE
       A7   D7   G
   LET IT SHINE, LET IT SHINE, LET IT SHINE

4. G
   SHINE ALL OVER THE WORLD

   I'M GONNA LET IT SHINE
   C
   SHINE ALL OVER THE WORLD
            G
   I'M GONNA LET IT SHINE

   SHINE ALL OVER THE WORLD
            B7   Em
   I'M GONNA LET IT SHINE
       A7   D7   G
   LET IT SHINE, LET IT SHINE, LET IT SHINE

5. LET IT SHINE TILL JESUS COMES

   I'M GONNA LET IT SHINE
   C
   LET IT SHINE TILL JESUS COMES
            G
   I'M GONNA LET IT SHINE

   LET IT SHINE TILL JESUS COMES
            B7   Em
   I'M GONNA LET IT SHINE
       A7   D7   G
   LET IT SHINE, LET IT SHINE, LET IT SHINE

I'VE GOT PEACE LIKE A RIVER

In this simple tune, the chord progression again expands beyond the basic three chords, adding the chords A7 and Em. The G changes to G7 pretty quickly; with the suggested fingerings, that change should come pretty easily with practice.

The chord progression in the last four measures of the melody (G–Em–A7–D7–G) is known as the I–vi–II–V (one–six–two–five) progression, which is the basis for many familiar tunes like "Blue Moon," "Heart and Soul," and "Since I Fell for You." Like the I–IV–V progression, the I–vi–II–V and its derivations are basic, common, and important progressions to get your head and hands around.

Hot licks master Roy Clark plays a rousing version of "I've Got Peace Like a River" on *Hymns from the Old Country Church* (Wonder Disk 61).

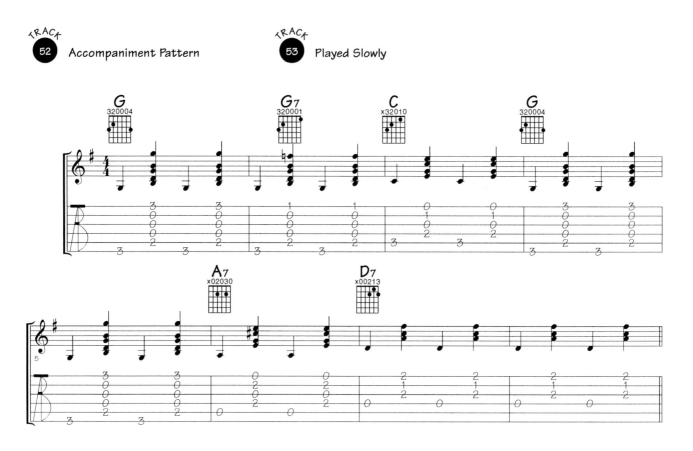

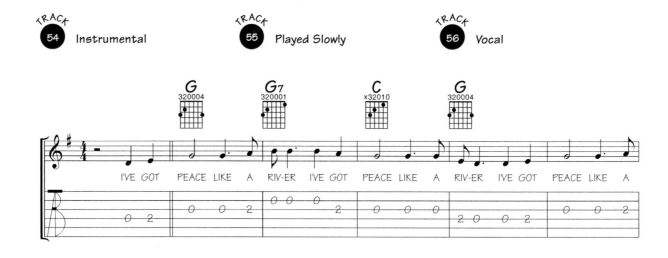

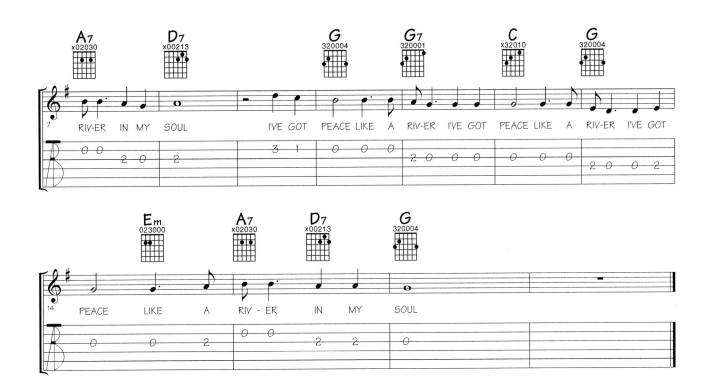

1. I'VE GOT PEACE LIKE A RIVER
```
       G            G7           C          G
1. I'VE GOT PEACE LIKE A RIVER, I'VE GOT PEACE LIKE A RIVER
                    A7           D7
   I'VE GOT PEACE LIKE A RIVER IN MY SOUL
       G            G7           C          G
   I'VE GOT PEACE LIKE A RIVER, I'VE GOT PEACE LIKE A RIVER
                 Em  A7  D7   G
   I'VE GOT PEACE LIKE A RIVER IN MY SOUL

                    G7            C           G
2. I'VE GOT LOVE LIKE AN OCEAN, I'VE GOT LOVE LIKE AN OCEAN
                    A7           D7
   I'VE GOT LOVE LIKE AN OCEAN IN MY SOUL
       G            G7           C           G
   I'VE GOT LOVE LIKE AN OCEAN, I'VE GOT LOVE LIKE AN OCEAN
                 Em  A7  D7   G
   I'VE GOT LOVE LIKE AN OCEAN IN MY SOUL

                    G7             C         G
3. I'VE GOT JOY LIKE A FOUNTAIN, I'VE GOT JOY LIKE A FOUNTAIN
                    A7            D7
   I'VE GOT JOY LIKE A FOUNTAIN IN MY SOUL
       G            G7            C          G
   I'VE GOT JOY LIKE A FOUNTAIN, I'VE GOT JOY LIKE A FOUNTAIN
                 Em   A7   D7    G
   I'VE GOT JOY LIKE A FOUNTAIN IN MY SOUL
```

SOMETIMES I FEEL LIKE A MOTHERLESS CHILD

Before the Civil War, slave children were often separated from their parents. One child, Ned Turner, had a rare visit from his mother. She gave him ginger cakes. That night he learned that he was somebody's child. There is nothing worse than a mother losing her child, or a child losing his mother. There is little comfort for this, but we can sing to relieve our stress and express our longing. Blues tunes, like gospel and spirituals, often lament the hard knocks of life. This great tune is in a similar vein as George Gershwin's

"Summertime"—in fact both are covered as a medley in a very soulful version by Mahalia Jackson (*Bless This House*, Columbia 8761). Original folkster Pete Seeger sings "Motherless Child" on *Folk Songs for Young People* (Smithsonian Folkways 45024).

This is our first song in a minor key, in this case Am. More specifically this song is referred to as a minor blues. Minor keys are often associated with sad moods and are common in blues and gospel laments.

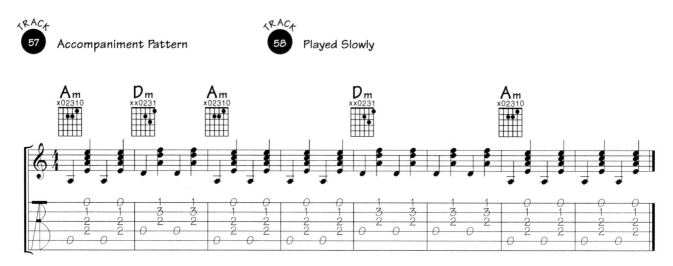

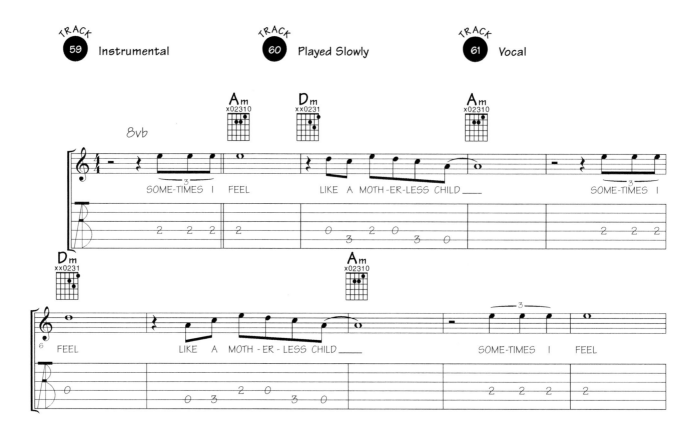

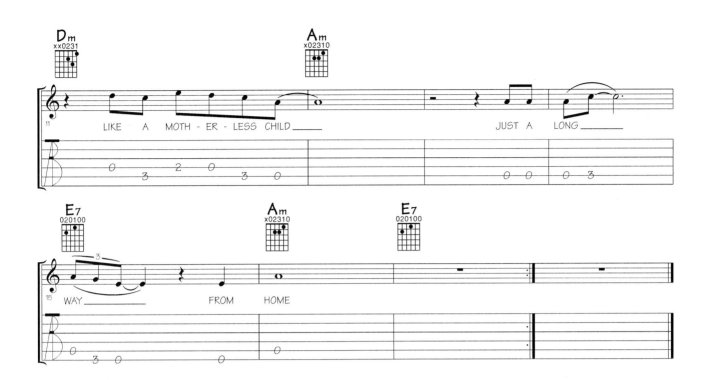

1. SOMETIMES I FEEL LIKE A MOTHERLESS CHILD
   SOMETIMES I FEEL LIKE A MOTHERLESS CHILD
   SOMETIMES I FEEL LIKE A MOTHERLESS CHILD
   JUST A LONG WAY FROM HOME

2. WISH I COULD FLY LIKE A BIRD IN THE SKY
   WISH I COULD FLY LIKE A BIRD IN THE SKY
   WISH I COULD FLY LIKE A BIRD IN THE SKY
   LITTLE CLOSER TO HOME

3. MOTHERLESS CHILDREN HAVE A REAL HARD TIME
   MOTHERLESS CHILDREN HAVE A REAL HARD TIME
   MOTHERLESS CHILDREN HAVE A REAL HARD TIME
   SO LONG, SO LONG, SO LONG

4. SOMETIMES I FEEL LIKE FREEDOM IS NEAR
   SOMETIMES I FEEL LIKE FREEDOM IS NEAR
   SOMETIMES I FEEL LIKE FREEDOM IS NEAR
   BUT WE'RE SO FAR AWAY

5. SOMETIMES I FEEL LIKE IT'S CLOSE AT HAND
   SOMETIMES I FEEL LIKE IT'S CLOSE AT HAND
   SOMETIMES I FEEL LIKE THAT FREEDOM IS NEAR
   BUT WE'RE SO FAR FROM HOME

WHEN JOHNNY COMES MARCHING HOME

Patrick Sarsfield Gilmore, an Irishman who came to America in 1848, before the potato famine, wrote the words to "Johnny," inspired by the tune of an old Irish folk song. Gilmore was regarded by John Philip Sousa as the "Father of the American Band." Gilmore is also credited with starting the tradition of bringing in the New Year with music at Times Square in New York City. During the Civil War, "Johnny" was sung in both the north and south to praise homecoming soldiers.

I've been familiar with this tune as far back as I can remember. The Mitch Miller version can be heard on

50 All-American Favorites (Sony 05162). For a sneak peek into the limitless possibilities of acoustic guitar, check out the modern rendition by master fingerstylist Alex de Grassi on *Now and Then: Folk Songs for the 21st Century* (33rd Street 3317).

"Johnny" is in the key of E minor but sometimes sounds as if it's in the key of G major. This ambiguity is common, because the two keys are closely related: Em is called the *relative minor* of G, and G is the *relative major* of Em. Every key has a relative major or minor.

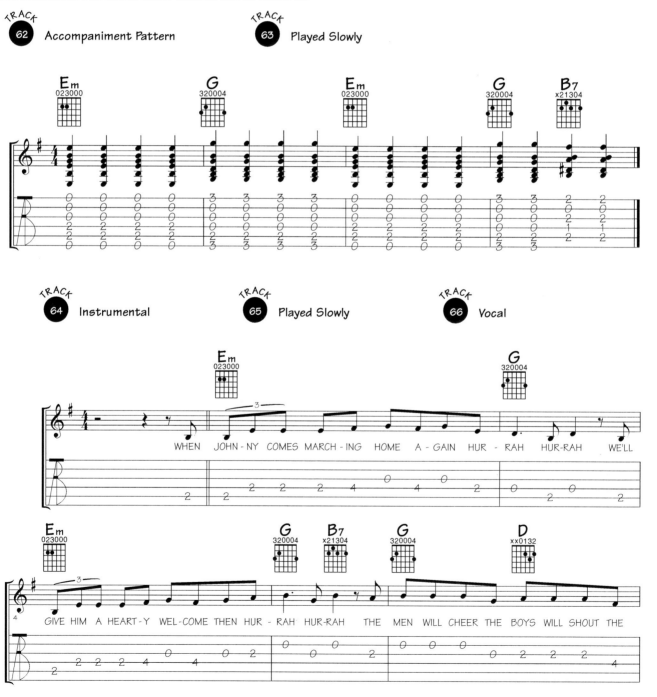

LAD-IES THEY__ WILL ALL TURN OUT AND WE'LL ALL FEEL GAY WHEN JOHN-NY COMES MARCH-ING HOME

1.
          Em
WHEN JOHNNY COMES MARCHING HOME AGAIN
   G
HURRAH! HURRAH!
       Em
WE'LL GIVE HIM A HEARTY WELCOME THEN
   G   **B7**
HURRAH! HURRAH!
   G   **D**
THE MEN WILL CHEER, THE BOYS WILL SHOUT
       Em   **B7**
THE LADIES THEY WILL ALL TURN OUT
          G   **B7**
AND WE'LL ALL FEEL GAY WHEN
Em   **Am**   **Em**
JOHNNY COMES MARCHING HOME

2.
THE OLD CHURCH BELLS WILL PEAL WITH JOY
   G
HURRAH! HURRAH!
   Em
TO WELCOME HOME OUR DARLING BOY
   G   **B7**
HURRAH! HURRAH!
    G   **D**
THE VILLAGE LADS AND LASSIES SAY
     Em   **B7**
WITH ROSES THEY WILL STREW THE WAY
      G   **B7**
AND WE'LL ALL FEEL GAY WHEN
Em   **Am**   **Em**
JOHNNY COMES MARCHING HOME

3.
GET READY FOR THE JUBILEE
   G
HURRAH! HURRAH!
   Em
WE'LL GIVE THE HERO THREE TIMES THREE
   G   **B7**
HURRAH! HURRAH!
    G   **D**
THE LAUREL WREATH IS READY NOW
    Em   **B7**
TO PLACE UPON HIS LOYAL BROW
      G   **B7**
AND WE'LL ALL FEEL GAY WHEN
Em   **Am**   **Em**
JOHNNY COMES MARCHING HOME

4.
LET LOVE AND FRIENDSHIP ON THAT DAY
   G
HURRAH! HURRAH!
   Em
THEIR CHOICEST TREASURES THEN DISPLAY
   G   **B7**
HURRAH! HURRAH!
    G   **D**
AND LET EACH ONE PERFORM SOME PART
    Em   **B7**
TO FILL WITH JOY THE WARRIOR'S HEART
      G   **B7**
AND WE'LL ALL FEEL GAY WHEN
Em   **Am**   **Em**
JOHNNY COMES MARCHING HOME

WHEN THE SAINTS COME MARCHING IN

This song is most commonly associated with Louis Armstrong, the father of New Orleans–style Dixieland jazz. The Beatles even did a cover of "Saints" in their early years. Flatt and Scruggs set the bluegrass standard with a smokin' rendition on *Flatt and Scruggs, 1964–1969* (Bear Family 15879).

"Saints" follows a three-chord progression (G, C, D7), with the G again moving to G7 in the latter part of the tune. As in "This Train," learn to feel the natural cycle of the G chord being played for four measures, then another two measures before the change to D7.

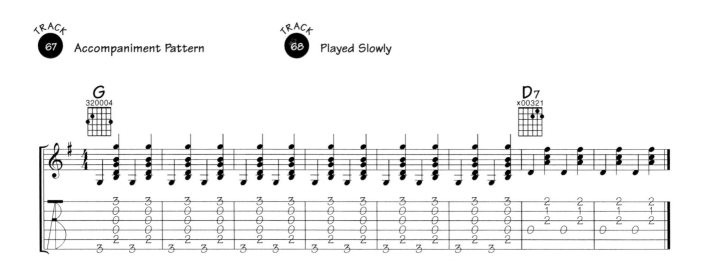

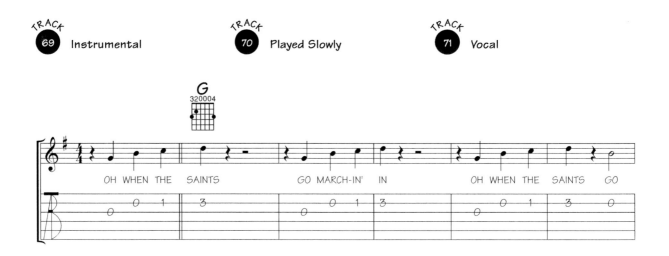

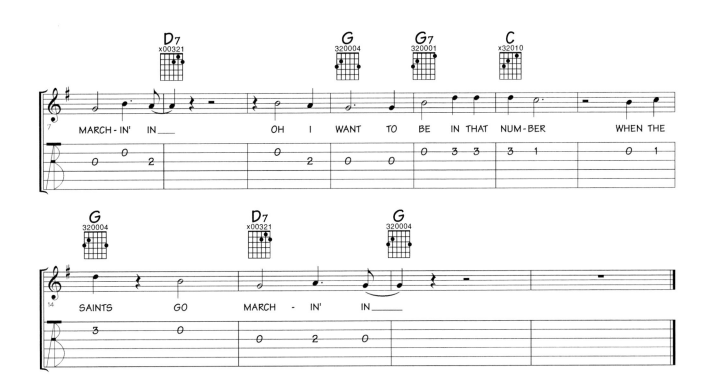

1. OH WHEN THE SAINTS *GO MARCHIN'* IN (G)
   OH WHEN THE SAINTS *GO MARCHIN'* IN (D7)
   OH I WANT TO BE IN THAT NUMBER (G / G7 / C)
   WHEN THE *SAINTS GO MARCHIN'* IN (G / D7 / G)

2. OH WHEN THE SUN BEGINS TO SHINE
   WHEN THE SUN BEGINS TO SHINE (D7)
   OH I WANT TO BE IN THAT NUMBER (G / G7 / C)
   WHEN THE *SAINTS GO MARCHIN'* IN (G / D7 / G)

3. OH WHEN THE HORN BEGINS TO SOUND (G)
   OH WHEN THE HORN BEGINS TO SOUND (D7)
   OH I WANT TO BE IN THAT NUMBER (G / G7 / C)
   WHEN THE SAINTS GO MARCHIN' IN (G / D7 / G)

4. OH WHEN THE DAY OF JUDGMENT COMES
   OH WHEN THE DAY OF JUDGMENT COMES (D7)
   OH I WANT TO BE IN THAT NUMBER (G / G7 / C)
   WHEN THE SAINTS GO MARCHIN' IN (G / D7 / G)

ROCK MY SOUL

Rock my soul, you made it to the end of the book! One of the challenges of musical study is the urge to bail out when self-doubt creeps in. Use this rousing tune as a reminder to push on toward success.

This song uses just two chords, D and A7, and is a great example of how two chords can be just as effective as three or more. The truth is, all you need is one. Even the V (A) is always pointing to the I (D), which conveniently houses the lyric "bosom of Abraham." Have your friends sing the response lines shown in parentheses.

Versions of this old spiritual seem to vary as much in melody as they do in title. The children's song "Skip to My Lou" bears some resemblance to the most common version of this song. Louis Armstrong rocks our soul on *Louis and the Angels/Louis and the Good Book* (MCA International 19379), and the Foxview Valley Boys perform a simple and peaceful version on *Mountain Music Featuring the Dulcimer* (King 5107).

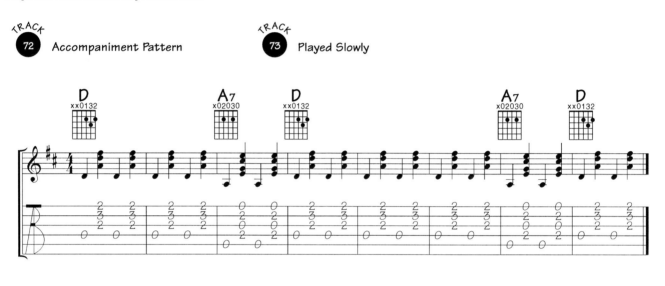

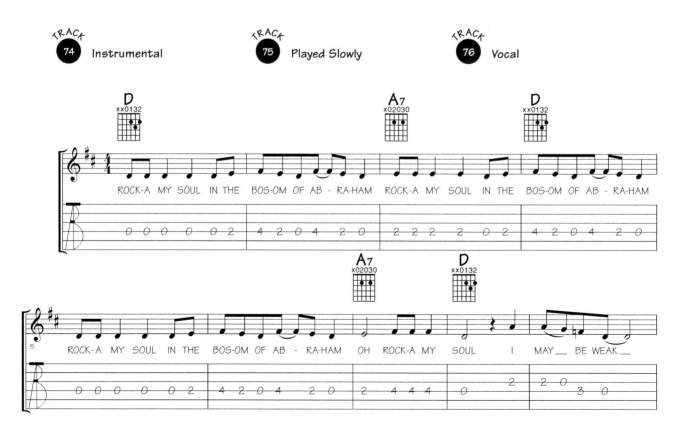

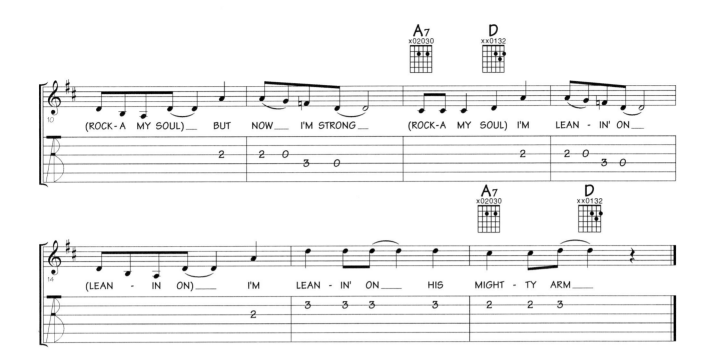

D
ROCK-A MY SOUL IN THE BOSOM OF ABRAHAM
A7   D
ROCK-A MY SOUL IN THE BOSOM OF ABRAHAM

ROCK-A MY SOUL IN THE BOSOM OF ABRAHAM
A7   D
OH, ROCK-A MY SOUL

1. I MAY BE WEAK (ROCK-A MY SOUL)
                          A7   D
    BUT NOW I'M STRONG (ROCK-A MY SOUL)

    I'M LEANIN' ON (LEANIN' ON)
                        A7   D
    I'M LEANIN' ON HIS MIGHTY ARM

        CHORUS

2. MY SOUL IS GLAD (ROCK-A MY SOUL)
                        A7   D
    MY SOUL IS FREE (ROCK-A MY SOUL)

    I'M GOIN' HOME (GOIN' HOME)
                        A7   D
    I'M GOIN' HOME TO LIVE WITH THEE

        CHORUS

3. MY SOUL IS GLAD (ROCK-A MY SOUL)
                        A7   D
    MY SOUL IS FREE (ROCK-A MY SOUL)

    I'M GOIN' HOME (GOIN' HOME)
                        A7   D
    I'M GOIN' HOME TO LIVE WITH THEE

        CHORUS

ABOUT THE AUTHOR

Peter Penhallow began playing piano and imitating Elvis Presley at the age of three, and he took up guitar at age nine. During the 13 years he was in the rock band Timmy, he cowrote and coproduced demos with Eddy Offord of Yes and Emerson, Lake, and Palmer; Andy West of the Dixie Dregs; and Vince Welnick of the Tubes and the Grateful Dead. He has played in recording sessions with Mark O'Connor, Huey Lewis band members Bill Gibson and Mario Cippolina, and many others. When he is not composing, accompanying, or improvising, he enjoys producing. Penhallow has been a musical director for Children's and Community Musical Theater in Marin County, California, for 25 years, and has more than a hundred productions to his credit. He also has four CDs for young children and is the author of *Christmas Songs for Beginning Guitar* and *Children's Songs for Beginning Guitar*.